Mathias Riechert

Measuring the Success of a Wiki for Small Organizations

GRIN Verlag

Bibliografische Information der Deutschen Nationalbibliothek:

Die Deutsche Bibliothek verzeichnet diese Publikation in der Deutschen National-
bibliografie; detaillierte bibliografische Daten sind im Internet über http://dnb.d-
nb.de/ abrufbar.

Imprint:

Copyright © 2011 GRIN Verlag GmbH
Druck und Bindung: Books on Demand GmbH, Norderstedt Germany
ISBN: 978-3-640-91238-4

This book at GRIN:

http://www.grin.com/en/e-book/171757/measuring-the-success-of-a-wiki-for-small-
organizations

GRIN - Your knowledge has value

Der GRIN Verlag publiziert seit 1998 wissenschaftliche Arbeiten von Studenten, Hochschullehrern und anderen Akademikern als eBook und gedrucktes Buch. Die Verlagswebsite www.grin.com ist die ideale Plattform zur Veröffentlichung von Hausarbeiten, Abschlussarbeiten, wissenschaftlichen Aufsätzen, Dissertationen und Fachbüchern.

Visit us on the internet:

http://www.grin.com/

http://www.facebook.com/grincom

http://www.twitter.com/grin_com

TECHNISCHE UNIVERSITÄT DRESDEN

Faculty of Business and Economics

Seminar Paper

Winter Term 2011

Measuring the Success of a Wiki for Small Organizations

Name: Mathias Riechert

Submission Date: 24th March, 2011

Table of Contents

List of Figures

List of Tables

List of Abbrevations

A	Attitude toward Using
BI	Behavioral Intention
b_i	Beliefs
D&M	Information Success Model of DeLone & McLean
DW	Data Warehouse
e_i	Evaluations
EOU	Perceived Ease of Use
HTML	Hypertext Markup Language
IS	Information System
IT	Information Technology
KM	Knowledge Management
KMS	Knowledge Management System
KS	Knowledge Sharing
mc_i	Motivation to comply
nb_i	Normative Beliefs
SCT	Self-Categorization Theory
SN	Subjective Norm
TAM	Technology Acceptance Model
TRA	Theory of Reasoned Action
U	Perceived Usefulness
WYSIWYG-editor	What You See Is What You Get editor

1   Introduction

1.1   Problem Definition and Objectives

The impact of knowledge management systems (KMS) on organizations grows rapidly. Increasingly, corporations are also using wikis to support employee collaboration and knowledge management (cf. Wagner, 2004, p. 104). A 2008 study by Gartner indicates that this year half of all US companies will use wikis (Morse, 2008). Wikis allow open collaboration in organizations and offer great potential for teamwork and knowledge management (KM). Using this potential for organizations in research context is a difficult task, because user groups are smaller and many tools already exist. It is therefore crucial to understand what makes a wiki successful. This seminar paper investigates the success factors of wikis derived from practical surveys, classifies them for relevance to small organizations and finally builds a wiki success model based on IS research and the practical success factors found.

Research Questions:

[1] What success factors for wikis are described in practical context?

[2] How important are they for small organizations in the research context?

[3] How can these factors be applied to a wiki success model adapted from IS success research?

1.2   Course of Investigation

This seminar paper starts with discussing the wiki concept in chapter 2. In order to build a success model, wiki success factors from practical background are derived from surveys. The resulting factors are evaluated in chapter 2.2.

Chapter 3 first introduces basic IS success models. Afterwards adapted models in the knowledge management system and knowledge sharing context are analyzed. The focus lies on pointing out changes to the model structure, discussing the results of empirical validation and evaluating the possible adaption for a wiki success model.

Based on these results the model is presented in chapter 4. This covers the process of modeling as well as a detailed variable and hypothesis discussion. The chapter closes with a concluding systematization of the proposed variables, measures and hypotheses.

The last chapter concludes the findings, discusses limitations of the paper, and gives implication for future research.

2   Wiki Success for Small Organizations

2.1   Wiki Characteristics

Wikis were introduced by Ward Cunningham in 1994, under the name WikiWikiWeb (Leuf & Cunningham, 2001, p. 3). In Hawaiian the word "wikiwiki" means "quick". „A WikiWikiWeb (aka wiki) is an open source collaborative server technology that enables users to access, browse, and edit hypertext pages in a real-time context" (Leuf & Cunningham, 2001, p. 442). "This makes a wiki a simple and easy-to-use platform for cooperative work on texts and hypertexts" (Ebersbach, Glaser, Heigl, & Warta, 2007, p. 12).

The aim of wikis is to create a set of dynamically linked pages. A simple markup language is used to connect the linked words to new pages. This process does not require a deep technical knowledge and can be accomplished easily. The nature of this idea leads to the necessity of the existence of a user group willing to contribute individual knowledge to a shared knowledge base. Kousetti (2008, p. 1) and Schaffert (2006, p. 1 f.) describe the following key characteristics of Wikis:

- **Easy Editing:**
  The content can be edited in a browser, resulting in minimal technical requirements. No additional client software has to be installed. The navigation, access and update of Wiki content is easy and can be conducted from the contributor's point of access (cf. Ebersbach et al., 2007, p. 15).

- **Simplified Wiki Syntax:**
  Wiki systems use a simplified hypertext format that is easy to learn and use for non-technical users. No knowledge of HTML is required. However, most Wikis enable the integration of more complex content via HTML or Widgets. As markup constructs are necessary for linking and embedding more complex content; limited expertise is required (cf. Schaffert, 2006, p. 1).

- **Rollback Mechanism:**
  Every change in the content is versioned and previous versions of the content are kept. This allows for an easy rollback in case of an accidental deletion or undesirable modification. Many Wikis offer comparison for tracking changes in the content.

- **Unrestricted Access:**
  Every user of a wiki can create, edit and delete content (cf. Back, Gronau, & Tochtermann, 2008, p. 11). This leads to the necessity of change management, which is supported by the rollback mechanisms described above. Many Wiki systems provide access restrictions based on rules or user groups. This enables more complex wiki types with private subgroups and public pages in one Wiki.

- **Collaborative Editing:**
  The described characteristics enable the work of many contributors to one central knowledge base. Furthermore many Wikis provide additional tools like discussion forums, summaries of changes, and list of updates.

- **Strong Linking:**
  The easy Wiki syntax allows for pages to be connected by links easily. New pages can be created by linking a so far not existing page and clicking on the link. Additionally the links can be used in reverse to find pages referring to the actual page. The linking structure can be hierarchical or non-linear, depending on the wiki's complexity (cf. Ebersbach et al., 2007, p. 15).

- **Search Function:**
  To improve the navigation within the wiki almost all wikis allow search via keywords, tags, or full-texts.

2.2   Success Factors for Small Organizations

Due to the novelty of Wikis few surveys have been conducted on the success factors of wikis in practical context. Thus, the definitions for the success factors discussed in the literature are inconsistent. Maleh (2000, p. 38) and Ebersbach et al. (2007, p. 24) list the principles depicted in Table 1. The relevance for small organizations in research context is evaluated in the right columns and the table is sorted from high relevance to low relevance.

Table 1: Wiki Success Principles

Principle	Description in (Ebersbach et al., 2007, p. 24 ff.)	Relevance for small organizations[1]	
Writing behavior	The most common types of writing behavior are: Never Writing, Proofreading and Style Changes, Subject Experts and Generalists.	Tracking the writing behavior is very important, because with few people writing a higher percentage has to contribute to make the wiki successful.	high
Playful creation	The loose playful atmosphere and fun at work are important conditions for self-organized processes, because creative, social and practical skills can best be unfolded.	Very important to increase motivation.	high
Diversity of the participants	A climate of openness and mutual trust is necessary – despite inevitable conflicts. Every user is initially recognized as an expert.	Incorporating the different views and aims in the common culture of trust and sharing is crucial in small workgroups.	high
Self-determined work	Cooperation in open wiki projects is attractive because strategies, focal points, and work intensity can be self-determined to a large extend.	Self-determined work is important to increase user satisfaction; nevertheless, consistent use of terminology is important.	high

---

[1] The relevance is evaluated based on the answers of a survey on KM in the form of expert interviews at the chair of Information Systems in January 2011.

Principle	Description in (Ebersbach et al., 2007, p. 24 ff.)	Relevance for small organizations[1]	
Modification pressure	The pressure to modify (as intrinsic motivation) and the will to solve a problem represent an indispensable motor.	This "pressure" can be addressed in a knowledge culture. In Science context the "problem to solve" can be project milestones, shared publications, or research steps.	medium
Extremely flexible scheduling	It is possible to suit one's own rhythm and individual daily life. Time pressure arises only when problems remain untouched.	Scheduling in small scientific organizations is more flexible than in large companies. However, there is few spare time. Therefore efficient scheduling is vital.	medium
Reception behavior	Number of visits, reading depth, search behavior is the aim of assessment.	In small user groups the measurement of reception requires more effort than benefit is generated.	medium
Social behavior	Social behavior refers to the form in which criticism and encouragement are imparted.	Having a good culture of sharing improves user satisfaction. Still, the benefits of good culture are higher with a large contributor group.	medium
Flat hierarchies	The responsibility for the entire process is transferred completely to those individuals performing in that process.	In small groups of employees hierarchies are not as important as in large company wikis. The remaining hierarchies play a secondary role in the wiki culture.	low
Simple system, simple rules	Wiki technology, with its low technical access hurdles, is ideal for web-based group processes. Several wiki communities have implemented simple codes of conduct.	In research context, the user group is smaller and easier to train. More complex types of content (Diagrams, References, Tables, etc.) are essential for a scientific collaboration wiki, leading to a higher complexity.	low
Open access	The success of the wiki philosophy is based on the fact that discussions are removed from alleged expert and specialist circles, right from the start. This creates transparency and incentive.	Because the knowledge stored is very valuable, role models are necessary to ensure the right user groups having access. Inside the groups, all forms of interaction with the wiki have to be allowed.	low
Structural behavior	People in self-organized processes ideally receive functions through their authority and the trust they have earned through their work.	Organization and administration is more important for large contributor groups, because more editing conflicts emerge there.	low

The field study by Grudin & Poole (2010, p. 4 ff.) compares Wiki success in six companies and derives the following success factors:

- **Aligning the expectations of managers and individual contributors:**
  The goal is to minimize the mismatch between managerial vision and the practices of individual contributors. Hierarchies in the company must be disrupted to solve this problem, because open collaboration and a "Culture of Sharing" are crucial for the success of the Wiki (cf. Grudin & Poole, 2010, p. 4).
- **Content organization and flexibility over time:**
  The organization of the content gets difficult when Wikis have to be merged, because there are many redundant page names. The usage of namespaces enables different Wikis to get combined, but makes searching for consistent information more difficult.
- **Positioning the wiki in an existing information ecology and corporate culture:**
  Existing communication and collaboration technologies will get disrupted by a tool based on a fundamentally different participation style (cf. Grudin & Poole, 2010, p. 6). Because Wikis are just one option it is crucial to differentiate it to the existing tools. Another problem is the *"Uncertainty about Editing Others' Work"*. Concerns over disrupting culture around ownership and accountability must be addressed by clearly defining the culture of sharing. Because *"Wikis are Ill-suited for Some Tasks"* Wiki platforms need to be developed further to include more complex content like diagrams or more formatting.

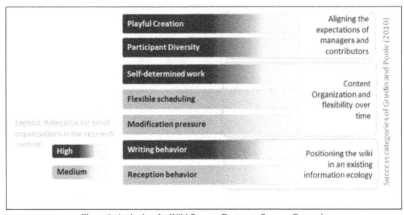

Figure 1: Assigning the Wiki Success Factors to Success Categories

Figure 1 assigns the success factors discussed in Table 1 to the three success factors of Grudin & Poole (2010, p. 4 ff.). Only high and medium relevance factors are integrated in order to keep the complexity low. This mapping is adapted for small organizations in the scientific environment. The resulting success factors will be used in the modeling of a wiki success model in chapter 0.

3   Success Measurement Model

3.1   Information System Success

Figure 2 depicts the different levels of IS success. The definition of success of an Information System (IS) depends on the position of the critic. A business manager requires economic results like "improved turnover", or "cost savings" in order to acknowledge the IS's success. This view is represented by the organizational level in Figure 2. The next level aims at reducing process cycle times or process costs. For staff members an IS may be successful if it is simplifying access to knowledge, even if no benefit is directly measurable. This can be taken into account by rating success on the user level. It is possible to consider the system usage or the user satisfaction to evaluate the success.

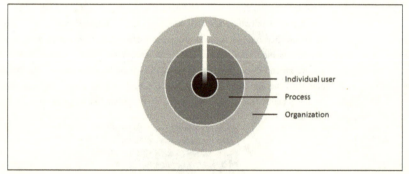

Figure 2: Levels of IS Succes

System usage is defined as "the utilization of information technology (IT) by individuals, groups, or organizations" (Robey, 1979, p. 527; Sharda, Barr, & McDonnell, 1988, p. 139; Straub, Limayem, & Karahanna-Evaristo, 1995, p. 1328). It is a necessary, albeit insufficient, requisite for deriving the benefits of IT. Accordingly, the IS's value increases with intensity of usage and number of users. However, this disregards the individual perception of usefulness. Users may use the system although there is no success for the company (cf. Davis, Bagozzi, & Warshaw, 1989, p. 1000). Furthermore this approach is not valid if the IS has to be used mandatory. To solve this problem it is possible to focus on user satisfaction. It has primary influence if the system is used mandatory (cf. Powers & Dickson, 1971, p. 156). Based on these three levels basic theories are discussed in the following.

3.2   Related Basic Theories

Understanding why people accept or reject systems has proven to be one of the most challenging issues in information systems (IS) research (cf. Swanson, 1974, p. 178). The influence factors were discussed controversially in the literature. Davis et al. (1989, p. 983) lists 21 different researchers working in that field of science from 1975 till 1987 alone. The lack of a common theoretical background resulted in a variety of mixed and inconclusive research findings (cf. Davis et al., 1989, p. 983).

To provide a brief overview over important theories, the original models of TRA, TAM and D&M are described in the following chapters.

3.2.1   Theory of Reasoned Action (TRA)

Davis et al. (1989, p. 983 ff.) introduced the usage of suggested intention models from social psychology as theoretical foundation for IS's success measurement. The "Theory of Reasoned Action" (TRA) (Ajzen & Fishbein, 1980; Fishbein & Ajzen, 1975) has proven successful in predicting and explaining behavior across a wide variety of domains (cf. Davis et al., 1989, p. 2). TRA is very general, "designed to explain virtually any human behavior" (Icek & Martin, 1980, p. 4).

Figure 3 depicts the TRA. This social psychology theory implies that a person's performance of a specified behavior is determined by his or her *behavioral intention* (BI). To measure BI, the *attitude toward the behavior* (A) and *subjective norm* (SN) are jointly determined. The weights are estimated by regression using the formula BI=A + SN.

The *attitude* is determined by the *beliefs* (b_i) about consequences of performing the behavior multiplied by the evaluation (e_i) of the consequences (cf. Fishbein & Ajzen, 1975, p. 216). The *subjective norm* is a multiplicative function of the person's *normative beliefs* (nb_i), i.e., perceived expectations of specific referent individuals or groups, and his or her motivation to comply (mc_i) with these expectations (Fishbein & Ajzen, 1975, p. 302).

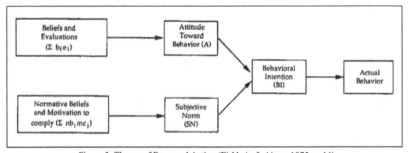

Figure 3: Theory of Reasoned Action (Fishbein & Ajzen, 1975, p. 16)

3.2.2   Technology Acceptance Model (TAM)

The Technology Acceptance Model (TAM) was introduced by Davis et al. (1985). It adapts the previously discussed TRA to model user acceptance of information. TAM's goal is to provide a simple and theoretically justified explanation of the determinants of computer acceptance systems (cf. Davis et al., 1989, p. 985). The posit is that that two particular beliefs, perceived usefulness and perceived ease of use, are of primary relevance for computer acceptance behaviors.

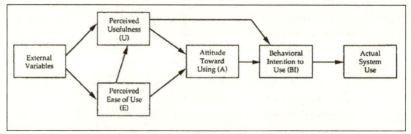

Figure 4: Technology Acceptance Model (TAM) (Davis et al., 1989, p. 985)

Figure 4 depicts the Technology Acceptance Model. As in Figure 3, the System use is determined by the *behavioral intention to use* (BI). BI itself depends on the *attitude toward using"* (A) and the *perceived usefullness* (U). Similar to TRA, BI's weights are estimated by regression with the formula: $BI = A + U$.

The SN is left out, because it is one of least understood aspects of TRA (cf. Fishbein & Ajzen, 1975, p. 304). Davis et al. (cf. Davis et al., 1989, p. 986) argue, that indirect effects of SN on BI are hard to disentangle from the indirect effects of A on BI. The A-BI relationship is fundamental to TRA and is retained. The U-BI relationship is based on the idea that people form intentions toward behaviors they believe will increase their job performance independently of positive or negative feelings evoked toward the behavior. Achieving various rewards like pay increases and promotions is abetted by enhanced performance (cf. Davis et al., 1989, p. 986). **Perceived usefulness** (U) means the users subjective probability that using a specific application system will increase his or her job performance within an organizational context. **Perceived ease of use** (EOU) refers to the degree to which the prospective user expects the target system to be free of effort. External variables are used to measure influences like system features or user characteristics. In contrast to TRA, where all beliefs (b_i) multiplied by corresponding evaluation weights (e_i) are summed up, TAM treats U and EOU as two fundamental and distinct constructs, allowing for the comparison of relative influence.

The model is the result of an empirical study conducted in 1989. The study comprises the answers of 107 students using word processing software on a voluntary basis. Three constructs are relevant for explaining usage behavior: *Behavioral intention, perceived usefulness*, and *perceived ease of use* (cf. Davis et al., 1989, p. 997). The exclusion of SN was confirmed (cf. Davis et al., 1989, p. 998). Further studies (Legris, Ingham, & Collerette, 2003, p. 192; Venkatesh & Davis, 2000, p. 186) prove TAM to predict about 40% of a system's use.

3.2.3   Information Systems Success Model of DeLone & McLean

The DeLone&McLean (D&M) model is a comprehensive, multidimensional model of IS success (cf. DeLone & McLean, 2003, p. 10) and intends to solve the problem of reducing the complexity of many different measurements. DeLone and McLean argue that information can be measured on different levels. This includes the technical, semantic and the effectiveness level (cf. Weaver, 1949, p. 2). These levels are the main categorization framework for measurement classification. DeLone and McLean adapt the categories assigned by Mason (1978) for IS Success. Figure 5 depicts the levels with the corresponding IS success categories.

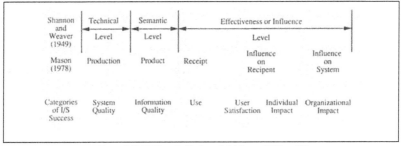

Figure 5: D&M Levels (DeLone & McLean, 1992, p. 62)

For each of the Categories surveys are compared to list different influence factors. *System quality* includes all measurements of the information processing system itself. *Information quality* contains ratings of IS output. *Information use* reflects the recipient's consumption of the output of an IS. *User satisfaction* measures the recipient's response to the use of the output of an IS. *Individual impact* contains the effect of information on the behavior of the recipient. *Organizational impact* is the effect of information on organizational performance (cf. DeLone & McLean, 1992, pp. 64-78).

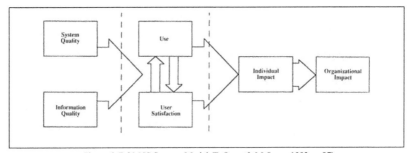

Figure 6: D&M IS Success Model (DeLone & McLean, 1992, p. 87)

DeLone and McLean postulate the categories to be independent and correlated to each other. In the "Ten-Year-Update" many consequential studies are listed (cf. DeLone & McLean, 2003, pp. 12-15). All of the interrelations are found to be significant by most of the studies. Later empirical field studies challenged or validated and supported the model. The relationships are casual, meaning that the increase of one category results in the increase of the caused one.

3.2.4 Model Suitability for Wikis in Small Organizations

The decision which theory to found the work on cannot be conducted based on literature alone. This is because Lee, Kozar and Larsen postulate TAM to be the most influential and commonly employed theory in IS (cf. Lee, Kozar, & Larsen, 2003, p. 752), while Smolnik, Urbach, Zimmer and Raeth indicate the D&M model to be the dominant one for measuring IS success (cf. Smolnik, Urbach, Zimmer, & Raeth, 2009, p. 1; Urbach, Smolnik, & Riempp, 2009, p. 321). Both TAM and D&M outlived their usefulness in the original version (cf. Benbasat, Barki, & Montréal, 2005, p. 214). There are many adaptions and revisions for both models available. This results in the reoccurrence of the original problem these models. There is no consistent basic theory for measuring IS success accepted by all scientists. While the TAM focuses on expectations of net benefits from future IS use, the D&M success model focuses on net realized benefits associated with IS use (cf. Y. Wang, 2008, p. 546).

The D&M model is chosen as the foundation of the further investigation because it includes user acceptance, which is crucial for wikis[2] being social software.

3.3 Adapted Models

Based on the models shown in chapter 3.1, adapted and revised models, relevant for wikis in small organizations, are discussed. The focus lies on the D&M model domain. Each model is analyzed for constructs that are relevant for the success factors discussed for wikis (Table 1, p. 3). The analysis focuses on the modeling changes and empirical results of significance. At first the updated D&M model is presented. Subsequently an adaption from the Data Warehousing domain is discussed. After that models from the Knowledge Management System (KMS) domain with D&M foundation are analyzed. Finally KMS models without a D&M foundation are presented. For all models with KMS and knowledge sharing (KS) context the transfer of the adaption for wiki systems is discussed.

Author	Year	Context	Basic Model			Chapter
			D&M	TAM	SCT	
Updated D&M	2002	IS	x			3.3.1
Nelson & Todd	2005	DW	x			3.3.2
Clay, Dennis, & Ko	2005	KMS	x			3.3.3
Wu & Wang	2006	KMS	x			3.3.4
Kulkarni	2007	KMS	x			3.3.5
Bock & Kim	2002	KS		x		3.3.6
Hsu, Ju, Yen, & Chang	2007	KS			x	3.3.6
Hsu & Lin	2008	KS		x		3.3.6

---

[2] See Table 1.

Figure 7: Analyzed Models

3.3.1   Updated D&M IS Success Model (2003)

DeLone and McLean published a ten year update for the D&M model in 2003 (DeLone & McLean, 2003). The article concluded empirical validating research on the model and modified the model based on the results of the research findings. The goal is to better reflect the changed role and management of IS (cf. DeLone & McLean, 2003, p. 23).

In the past twenty years the impacts have moved beyond the individual user (cf. DeLone & McLean, 2003, p. 19), making new variables for larger groups of impact necessary. To reduce the resulting complexity the constructs *individual impact* and *organizational impact* are combined together into one single variable *net benefits*, grouping all impacts together. The updated model introduces *service* as a new dimension of quality to reflect the changed IS-provider role as service provider (cf. DeLone & McLean, 2003, p. 18). In order to resolve some of the process vs. casual concerns raised by Seddon (1997, p. 251), the multidimensional nature of *use* is included in the model. This is achieved by allowing the measure to be alternatively *intention to use* as an attitude or *use* as behavior. The arrows added demonstrate proposed associations in a process sense, and can be positive or negative (cf. DeLone & McLean, 2003, p. 24). Figure 8 depicts the updated D&M IS success model.

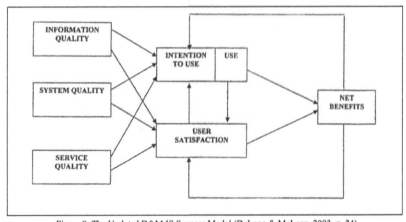

Figure 8: The Updated D&M IS Success Model (DeLone & McLean, 2003, p. 24)

Results: Nearly all empirical field studies conducted in the time between the original model and the changed one confirm the significance of the relationships between the variables. Only *system use – organizational impact* (Yoon, Guimaraes, & Clevenson, 1998) and *system quality – system use* (Goodhue & Thompson, 1995) were found to be not significant for some cases. The critique from Seddon (1997) lead to the distinction of *intention to use* and *use* as attitude and process variable. The newly introduced *service quality* is not empirically tested by DeLone and McLean in this study.

3.3.2 Success Model by Nelson & Todd (2005)

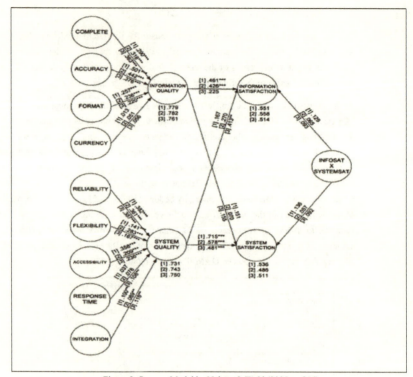

Figure 9: Success Model by Nelson & Todd (2005, p. 216)

Figure 9 depicts the IS success model of Nelson & Todd (2005). The goal of this model is to measure the success of Data Warehousing applications. To model this success Nelson and Todd refer to theoretical models postulating *information quality* and *system quality* as the key initial antecedents (DeLone & McLean, 1992; Mason, 1978; Seddon, 1997; Shannon & Weaver, 1997). Quality constructs for IS are multidimensional (Klein, 2003; Seddon, 1997). Nelson's model includes two of these dimensions, information and system quality.

In the context of Data Warehousing *information quality* is defined in the meaning of data quality and its measures focus on the technical aspect. They are derived from the categorization of intrinsic, contextual, and representational dimensions provided by Wang and Strong (1996, p. 18). Used dimensions are accuracy, completeness, currency, and format. The measures for *system quality* are closely related to service quality and ease of use (cf. Nelson & Todd, 2005, p. 205). The dimensions accessibility, reliability, response, flexibility, and integration are used.

Results: All relationships are significant, and explained a substantial portion of the variance (75 percent for information quality and 74 percent for system quality) (cf. Nelson & Todd, 2005, p. 222). However, the explanation power is limited because net benefits are excluded.

3.3.3   KMS Success Model by Clay et al. (2005)

The success model of Clay et al. (2005) is designed for the knowledge management system (KMS) context. It adapts the D&M model for the basic structure, but uses perceived *ease of use* instead of *user satisfaction* and *loyal use* instead of *net benefits*. These constructs are similar to the TAM (described in chapter 3.2.2, p. 8). Furthermore *extrinsic motivation* and *perceived voluntariness* are introduced to measure the success. *Loyal use* is a type of future use in which use of the technology has become part of the user's routine (cf. Oliver, 1999, p. 33). *Knowledge quality* is defined as the degree to which the knowledge contained in a KMS is useful in assisting the user in accomplishing tasks, independent of the KMS in which it is contained (cf. Clay et al., 2005, p. 3). Figure 10 depicts the model.

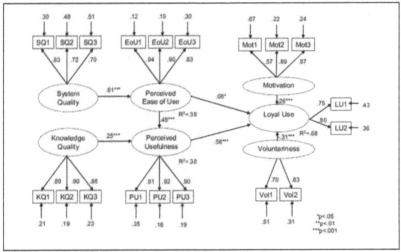

Figure 10: Success Model by Clay et al. (2005)

Results: Loyal Use of KMS was found to be directly and significantly affected by four factors (*perceived usefulness, voluntariness, extrinsic motivation, perceived ease of use*) and indirectly by two factors (*system quality, knowledge quality*). *Perceived Usefulness* has the highest influence on the use, *perceived ease of use* is significant, but has nearly no influence (cf. Clay et al., 2005, p. 7f.).

Wiki adaption: The model is adapted for KMS by focusing on *loyal use* and *knowledge quality* in the model. The usage is defined as "consumption of knowledge content" (cf. Clay et al., 2005, p. 2). Nevertheless, the model disregards the knowledge sharing aspect.

3.3.4 KMS Success Model by Wu & Wang (2006)

The success model of Wu and Wang (2006) uses the same constructs as the D&M model. However, changes regarding the variable definition and structure are incorporated. *Net benefits* are evaluated by *perceived benefits* (or perceived usefulness), because of intangible system impacts and intervening environmental variables result in numeric cost measures not being usable (cf. Wu & Y. M. Wang, 2006, p. 730). Wu and Wang criticize, that the right hand side of the D&M model has not been authenticated. The empirical validation of Seddon (1997) raised the confusion because of mixed process and casual explanation of IS success. Seddon further states, that *system use* precedes system benefits, but it does not cause them. This is the reason why Wu and Wang define system use as a behavior that reflects an expectation of system benefits from using an IS. Thus, *benefits* and *system use* are changed in their order. Figure 11 depicts the resulting model.

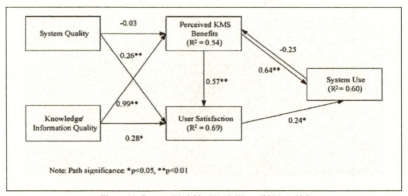

Figure 11: Success Model by Wu & Wang (2006, p. 736)

KMS success depends on the degree of *use* (cf. Poston & Speier, 2005, p. 224), which is tied to *system quality, information quality, user satisfaction,* and *usefulness. Knowledge / information quality* is a multi-dimensional construct having the two components content quality and context and linkage quality. Content quality is measured similar to other IS environments. The linkage is measured by an 11-item instrument developed by Wu and Wang (cf. Wu & Y. M. Wang, 2006, p. 732). *Perceived KMS benefits* are measured by the perception of the users.

Results: *KMS benefits* have a positive influence on *system use*, while the influence of *user satisfaction* is less significant. *System use* has a negative influence on *KMS benefits*. There is no significant relationship between *system quality* and *KMS benefits*. The relationship between *system quality* and *system use* proposed by other studies is not analyzed.

Wiki adaption: Like in the model of Clay (2005), *information quality* is modified. Instead of completely changing the items for knowledge context Wu and Wang introduce a multi-dimensional construct for *knowledge / information quality* and add the knowledge perspective to the content perspective. The measurement of *net benefits* by *perceived benefits* makes the measurement of this variable easier. The sharing aspect is included in *system use*.

3.3.5   KMS Success Model of Kulkarni (2007)

The model's goal is to incorporate the quality of available knowledge and KM systems and includes organizational support structure as a contributing factor (cf. Kulkarni, Ravindran, & Freeze, 2007, p. 309). Figure 12 depicts the model.

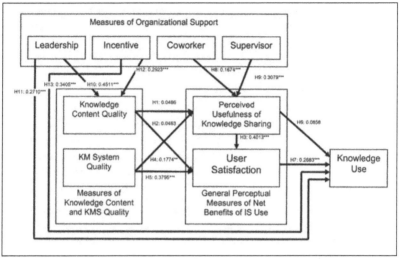

Figure 12: KMS Success Model by Kulkarni et al. (2007, p. 333)

Kulkarni also refers to Seddon (1997) stating that *use* is the consequence of IS success and not an intrinsic characteristic, and therefore is separated from the rest of the model. *System use* is substituted by *knowledge use*. *Perceived usefulness of knowledge sharing* replaces the *D&M IS use* variable.

Results: Ten of thirteen relationships analyzed are significant. Both *knowledge use* and *KM system quality* are significant and important determinants of *knowledge use* through their intermediate effect on *user satisfaction*. The organizational support variables have a significant positive effect on *knowledge use* (direct as well as indirect). The *perceived usefulness of knowledge sharing* is the only variable with insignificant relationships (*knowledge content quality, KM system quality. Perceived usefulness of knowledge sharing* only influences *knowledge use* with the SUR estimation results. Using LISREL this relationship is not significant, too.

Wiki adaption: The model implements knowledge adoption by using *knowledge content quality, KM system quality,* and *perceived usefulness of knowledge sharing* instead of the corresponding variables. The introduction of organizational support as a new group of variables is an interesting approach to measure sharing aspects, the resulting relationships are significant. However, the dimensions of the organizational variable are included as single variables, increasing the complexity of the model. This leads to more explanation power, for the price of scarcity.

3.3.6   Knowledge Sharing Research

Studies about knowledge sharing found their models on the TRA and the SCT. The research models are therefore not part of the analysis. However, the results of the studies are evaluated to examine if incorporating them into a Wiki success model offers advantages.

Bock & Kim (2002) found that the *rewards* variable is negatively related to the attitude of knowledge sharing. Thus, incentives do not create an enduring commitment to any action. For long-time effects they are ineffective. In contrast to that, *expected associations* and *contributions* have a positive effect on attitude toward knowledge sharing (cf. Bock & Kim, 2002, p. 19 f.).

Hsu, Ju, Yen, & Chang (2007) use the self-categorization theory (SCT) proposed by Bandura (1982) to analyze the influence on *knowledge sharing behavior*. The study found that *self-efficacy* plays a critical role in guiding individuals' behavior. *Personal outcome expectations* have significant influence on knowledge sharing behavior. Another result is that there are three levels of trust. *Economy-based trust* and *information-based trust* have to be established before *identification-based trust* can be developed. *Identification-based trust* plays a critical role in knowledge sharing behavior (cf. M. Hsu et al., 2007, p. 165 f.).

Hsu & Lin (2008) found *ease of use* and *enjoyment* to be important variables in the context of social software. *Perceived usefulness* has no effect on the usage. This is explained by *perceived usefulness* only being a critical factor in work-related environments (cf. C. L. Hsu & Lin, 2008, p. 71 f.).

Wiki adaption: The studies analyzed do focus more on the sharing aspect of social software than the KMS studies analyzed. *User-efficacy, user outcome expectations, trust, user enjoyment,* and *ease of use* have to be considered in wiki context, due to their influence on knowledge sharing. These findings are consistent to the identified success factors from the operational context discussed in chapter 2.2. Furthermore, the influence of *rewards* is rather short-termed, but can help triggering knowledge sharing in the initial phase (cf. Bock & Kim, 2002, p. 20). Finally, *perceived usefulness* has to be analyzed critically, because scientific research in small organizations is a work-related environment. Still, wikis have to be perceived as more useful as former used tools in order to be successive.

4 Adaption to Wiki Success

4.1 Wiki Success Model

The analysis of the existing research models for IS success revealed, that there are many ways to build a model for measuring the success of knowledge management tools or social software. Chapter 2.2 discussed success factors for wikis derived from practice. Compared to the variables derived from traditional IS theories, many terminological differences and inconsistences are existent. Starting point for building a model usable in practical context is the mapping of practical success factors to theoretically validated variables. This process influences the selection of variables for the proposed model.

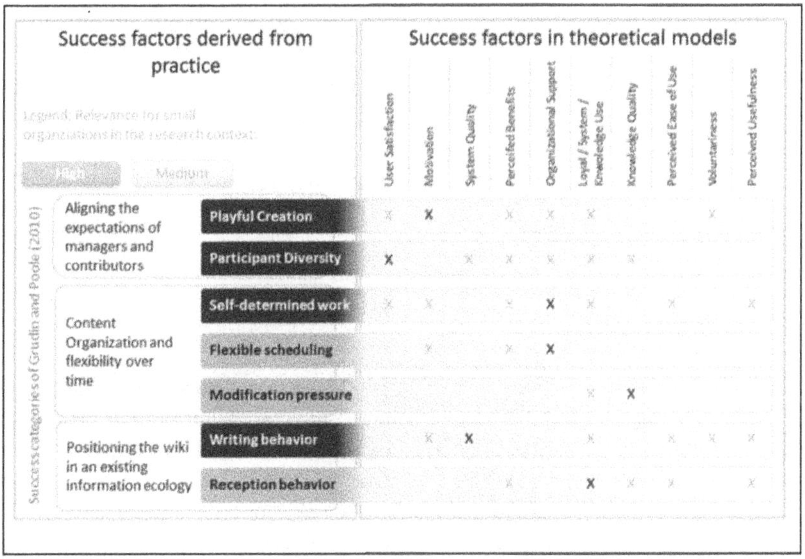

Success factors derived from practice		User Satisfaction	Motivation	System Quality	Perceived Benefits	Organizational Support	Loyal / System / Knowledge Use	Knowledge Quality	Perceived Ease of Use	Voluntariness	Perceived Usefulness
Aligning the expectations of managers and contributors	Playful Creation	x	X	x	x	x				x	
	Participant Diversity	x		x	x	x	x	x			
Content Organization and flexibility over time	Self-determined work	x	x		X	x			x		x
	Flexible scheduling	x			x	X					
	Modification pressure						x	X			
Positioning the wiki in an existing information ecology	Writing behavior	x	X			x			x	x	x
	Reception behavior				X	x	x	x			x

Legend: Relevance for small organizations in the research context: High / Medium

Figure 13: Success Factor Mapping

Figure 13 depicts the mapping. The practical factors are categorized on the left side. The importance evaluation is based on Table 1. The success factors with high and medium relevance for small organization in research context are grouped into the categories of Grudin and Poole (2010). The success factors derived from the theoretical models analyzed in chapter 3.3 are listed on the right side. This mapping has two goals:

- Indicating, which theoretical factors are important for this specific domain.
- Allocating the practical factors to the theoretically validated variables.

The crosses mark the allocations of the factors. As there are overlapping meanings there often is no single assignment possible. *Playful creation* for example is part of *user satisfaction* and *motivation*. Allocating the factors allows for them to be included as possible dimensions or items in the factors. In order to prevent redundant influence there has to be a distinct assignment. The highlighted crosses show the allocation that is most likely for wikis in research context. The evaluation again bases on the experiences of the analysis of a wiki in a research organization. Figure 13 shows, that all theoretical variables could be implemented. Nevertheless, the proposed wiki syntax model includes only elements of Wu and Wang (2006) and Clay et al. (2005) on variable level, to keep the model simple. Constructs of Kulkarni (2007) as well as knowledge sharing research is included on variable dimension and item level. Figure 14 depicts the proposed wiki success model's structure.

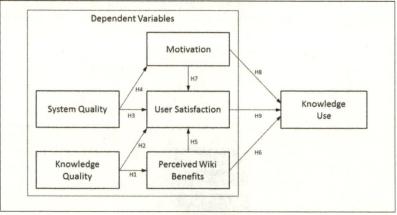

Figure 14: Wiki Success Model

Variables used: Based on Seddon's (1997) study, *use* is the consequence of IS success and not an intrinsic characteristic *use* is separated from the rest of the model; similar to Kulkarni's model (2007, p. 333). Furthermore it is changed to *knowledge use* to measure the usage of the knowledge provided by the wiki rather than only the usage. The benefits of the wiki are measured by using the *perceived wiki benefits*. This allows more authentic measurement. *Information quality* is changed to *knowledge quality. Motivation* is introduced to include other constructs like *motivation* (cf. Clay et al., 2005, p. 2)*, organizational support* (cf. Kulkarni et al., 2007, p. 333) and *enjoyment* (cf. C. L. Hsu & Lin, 2008, p. 71) as variable dimensions. *User satisfaction* is a central element for social software and was found to be significant by all studies discussed. Thus, it is included in the model for evaluating wiki success.

Variables not used: Kulkarni (2007) introduced the *perceived usefulness of knowledge sharing.* The empirical test showed that the only variable significantly influenced by that variable is *user satisfaction.* This is why *perceived usefulness of knowledge sharing* is not included as variable. *Perceived ease of use* was used by Clay (cf. 2005, p. 2). The empirical test showed that it has nearly no influence on use. Still, it is a useful dimension of *system quality.* The relationship between *system quality* and *perceived benefits* is insignificant (cf. Wu & Y. M. Wang, 2006, p. 736) and is therefore dropped. *Service quality* introduced by DeLone and McLean (2003) is dropped because service plays a minor role in small organizations; similar to Clay et al. (2005),

Kulkarni et al. (2007), Nelson & Todd (2005), Wu & Y. M. Wang (2006).

4.2   Variables

4.2.1   Knowledge Quality

Knowledge quality is adapted from the information quality variable of the D&M model. It is defined as the degree to which the knowledge contained in a wiki is useful in assisting the user in accomplishing tasks (cf. Clay et al., 2005, p. 3). Table 2 lists proposed measurement items described in the KMS related literature.

Table 2: Measurements Proposed for Knowledge Quality

Source	Clay et al., 2005, p. 10	Kulkarni et al., 2007, p. 326	Smolnik et al., 2009, p. 6
Usefulness	x	x	
Diversity	x		x
Relevance	x		
Presentation		x	x
Organization			x
Characteristics			x

Knowledge quality is measured with Usefulness, Diversity, Relevance and Characteristics are included in the wiki success model. Characteristics can include questions regarding the reception behavior (see Figure 13) to enquire reading depth or reading frequency.

Hypothesis 1: Higher level of *knowledge quality* leads to higher level of *perceived wiki benefits.*

> H1 was tested by Wu & Wang and found to be significant with a value of 0.99 (cf. Wu & Y. M. Wang, 2006, p. 736). It was found to be the main influence on perceived benefits.

Hypothesis 2: Higher level of *knowledge quality* leads to higher level of *user satisfaction.*

> H2 was tested by Kulkarni and Wu & Wang. They both found significant influence on *user satisfaction.* The values are 0.1774 (cf. Kulkarni et al., 2007, p. 333) and 0.28 (cf. Wu & Y. M. Wang, 2006, p. 736).

4.2.2   System Quality

System quality measures the operational characteristics. Smolnik et al. (2009, p. 6) identify the criteria Functionality, Accessibility, Task-technology, Integration, Ease of use, Reliability, Response time based on the criteria proposed by DeLone & McLean (2003). These measures are valid for the wiki context.

Hypothesis 3: Higher level of *system quality* leads to higher level of *user satisfaction*.

> This hypothesis was empirically tested by Wu & Wang and Kulkarni and found to be significant: $\beta = 0.26$ (Wu & Y. M. Wang, 2006, p. 736) and $\beta = 0.3795$ (Kulkarni et al., 2007, p. 333).

Hypothesis 4: Higher level of *system quality* leads to higher level of *motivation*.

> As *motivation* is a new construct, there are no empirical studies for validation yet. The reason for including this relationship lies in the factors like Ease of use, and Functionality to influence the motivation dimensions. These are described more detailed in chapter 4.2.4.

4.2.3   Perceived Wiki Benefits

Perceived system benefit was adapted by Wu & Wang defining it as the degree to which a user believes that use of the system results in benefits to the user or the organization (cf. Wu & Y. M. Wang, 2006, p. 731). The benefits of an IS need not to be financial, but can be soft and non-financial (cf. Holsapple & Joshi, 2000, p. 258). Because the benefits of social software are indirect, using perceptions of the users to measure provides soft indicators. Used criteria are knowledge storing, task efficiency, job performance, work life quality (cf. Wu & Y. M. Wang, 2006, p. 737).

Hypothesis 5: Higher level of *s perceived wiki benefits* leads to higher level of *user satisfaction*.

> This hypothesis was validated by Wu & Wang with $\beta = 0.57$ (cf. Wu & Y. M. Wang, 2006, p. 736).

Hypothesis 6: Higher level of *perceived wiki benefits* leads to higher level of *knowledge use*.

> H6 was validated with $\beta = 0.64$ (cf. Wu & Y. M. Wang, 2006, p. 736).

4.2.4   Motivation

The *motivation* measures the degree of support users provide. Clay (2005) linked it to *use*. Motivation can also be a subordinate for other constructs like knowledge sharing aspects (M. Hsu et al., 2007) and organizational support aspects (Kulkarni et al., 2007). The wiki success model therefore introduces two motivation dimensions: organizational motivation and sharing motivation. Measurements for the dimension organizational motivation: Incentive, Organizational Leadership, Recognition (cf. Kulkarni et al., 2007, p. 327). Measures for sharing motivation: Teamwork, Altruism, Enjoyability.

Hypothesis 7: Higher level of *motivation* leads to higher level of *user satisfaction*.

> This hypothesis was not subject of empirical tests yet.

Hypothesis 8: Higher level of *motivation* leads to higher level of *knowledge use*.

> Not directly validated. Still organizational motivation was validated by Kulkarni (2007), with leadership – use $\beta = 0.27$ and incentive – use $\beta = 0.34$.

4.2.5   User Satisfaction

User satisfaction is one of the most frequently measured aspects of IS success. Wu and Wang adapted the user satisfaction of the revised D&M model (2003) and found the indicators diverse knowledge need satisfaction, KMS efficiency, KMS effectiveness, KMS satisfaction overall (cf. Wu & Y. M. Wang, 2006, p. 737). The diverse knowledge need satisfaction enables the diversity discussed in the practical context to be considered in the model. The measurements are valid for wikis and therefore used in the model.

Hypothesis 9: Higher level of *user satisfaction* leads to higher level of *knowledge use*.

The studies conducted by Wu& Wang (2006) and Kulkarny (2007) both found signifiant influence on that hypothesis. $\beta = 0.24$ (Wu & Y. M. Wang, 2006) $\beta = 0.27$ (Kulkarni et al., 2007)

4.2.6   Knowledge Use

Due to the multifaceted meaning of the *use* variable (Seddon, 1997), it has to be defined explicitly in each model using it. In the provided context, *knowledge use* is the future degree of application of the knowledge provided by the wiki system. Table 3 lists the proposed knowledge use measurements.

Table 3: Measurements Proposed for Knowledge Use

Reference	Clay et al., 2005, p. 10	Kulkarni et al., 2007, p. 326	Smolnik et al., 2009, p. 6	(Wu & Y. M. Wang, 2006, p. 737)
Shared knowledge application	x	x		x
Knowledge classifyability		x		x
Knowledge sharing			x	x
Increased productivity			x	
Social impacts			x	
Information gain			x	
Future KM use	x			

Smolnik et al. and Wu & Wang propose to measure the knowledge sharing in the usage variable. The wiki success model approach differs from that in order to better measure the influence of sharing on success (via motivation). Including them two times could bring insights about how the present knowledge sharing improves the future knowledge use and sharing. Still, this might result in trivial significances. This is the reason why only Shared knowledge application, Knowledge classifyability, and Future wiki use are included. Thus, reception behavior (see Figure 13) is also considered.

Table 4: Variables Systematization

Measurements		Hypotheses[3]
Knowledge Quality	• Usefulness • Diversity • Relevance • Characteristics	H1: Higher level of knowledge quality leads to higher level of perceived wiki benefits. (β = 0.99) (Wu & Y. M. Wang, 2006). H2: Higher level of knowledge quality leads to higher level of user satisfaction. (σβ = 0.2287) (Kulkarni et al., 2007; Wu & Y. M. Wang, 2006)
System Quality	• Functionality • Accessibility • Task-technology • Integration • Ease of use • Reliability • Response time	H3: Higher level of system quality leads to higher level of user satisfaction. (σβ = 0.31975) (Kulkarni et al., 2007; Wu & Y. M. Wang, 2006) H4: Higher level of system quality leads to higher level of motivation. (not validated yet)
Perceived Benefits	• knowledge storing • task efficiency • job performance • work life quality	H5: Higher level of s perceived wiki benefits leads to higher level of user satisfaction. (β = 0.57) (Wu & Y. M. Wang, 2006, p. 736) H6: Higher level of perceived wiki benefits leads to higher level of knowledge use. (β = 0.64) (Wu & Y. M. Wang, 2006, p. 736)
Motivation	Organizational motivation: • Incentive • Organizational Leadership • Recognition Sharing motivation: • Teamwork • Altruism • Enjoyability.	H7: Higher level of motivation leads to higher level of user satisfaction. (not validated yet) H8: Higher level of motivation leads to higher level of knowledge use. (not directly validated, but single measurements have significant influence: leadership – use β = 0.27 and incentive – use β = 0.34) (Kulkarni et al., 2007, p. 333)
User Satisfaction	• diverse knowledge need satisfaction • Wiki efficiency • Wiki effectiveness	H9: Higher level of user satisfaction leads to higher level of knowledge use. (σβ = 0.255) (Kulkarni et al., 2007; Wu & Y. M. Wang, 2006)
Knowledge Use	• Shared Knowledge Application • Knowledge classifyability • Future wiki use	-

Table 4 gives an overview over the variables, their proposed measurements and the resulting hypotheses. The significance values given are drawn from the cited studies. They do not prove the relationship to be valid for wikis in small organizations, but give an indication on how significant the influence is for wikis in general. The empirical validation might result in different results for the weighting parameters. The relevant success factors derived from practical context are incorporated in the model.

---

[3] The median of previous empirical research results is included in brackets to give an indication about how distinct the influence of the hypothesis is.

5   Conclusion

5.1   Discussion and Limitations

[1] What success factors for wikis are described in practical context?

The wiki success factors in practical context are discussed in chapter 2.2. Table 1 lists success factors from practical context. Grudin & Poole (2010, p. 4 ff.) postulate a coarser definition for success categories. In order to get a consistent set of success factors, the success indicators from Table 1 are assigned to the categories in Figure 1.

[2] How important are they for small organizations in the research context?

The research context has different requirements according IS compared to large companies. The evaluation in Table 1 reflects these individual necessities by evaluating their relevance for small organizations. Thus, Table 1 answers research question [2].

[3] How can these factors be applied to a wiki success model adapted from IS success research?

The wiki success model is build based on an analysis of IS success models in the KMS and KS context. The variables derived in chapter 2.2 are mapped on the variables from the IS – models (Figure 13, p. 17). Thus, practical factors can be applied to build a model including both measurements types. The resulting model is depicted in Figure 14, p.18.

The evaluation process was conducted based on the key study experiences in a practical seminar in a research organization. The validity of the evaluation results is therefore limited. Empirical field studies are necessary to confirm or challenge the findings of this case. The mapping of practical success factors on theoretical validated success variables is imprecise, due to many possible combinations. Still there is a need for a distinct assignment in order to allow measurement items to be drawn from the mapping. A possible solution is modeling this mapping in a framework and using statistical methods to empirical validate relationships between the factors. A more automatable approach could be using artificial neuronal networks to automatically weight the relationships.

The analysis of the studies revealed that there are many different ways to model an information system. The provided model seeks to perform the balancing act between explanatory power and scarcity. Empirically validated concepts are combined in a new wiki success model. A new construct is introduced to involve the sharing motivation and organizational support motivation in a condensed form to keep the model simple. The appended measures are selected based on the requirements identified in chapter 2. The resulting model is adapted for wiki use in small companies and provides indications about expected significance for all hypotheses but the ones connecting the new motivation variable.

5.2   Future Research

Two main directions of future research are conceivable. Firstly, an empirical test has to validate the new model. This allows comparison to other models published in the literature. Additionally, measuring the relationships empirical would bring new findings regarding the construct *use* and its role and position in the evaluating a system's success, which is discussed controversially in the literature.

Secondly, the process of analyzing the success factors revealed a substantial terminological gap between theoretical constructs and practical needs. Due to the key study nature of the evaluation and mapping process the results are only of limited validity. Building a more formalized framework would allow for more general statements about dependencies.

Reference List

Ajzen, I., & Fishbein, M. (1980). *Understanding Attitudes and Predicting Social Behavior* (Facsimile.). Prentice Hall.

Back, A., Gronau, N., & Tochtermann, K. (2008). *Web 2.0 in der Unternehmenspraxis: Grundlagen, Fallstudien und Trends zum Einsatz von Social Software.* Oldenbourg Wissenschaftsverlag.

Bandura, A. (1982). Self-efficacy mechanism in human agency. *American psychologist, 37*(2), 122–147.

Benbasat, I., Barki, H., & Montréal, H. E. C. (2005). *Quo vadis TAM.* HEC Montréal, Chaire de recherche du Canada en implantation et gestion des technologies de l'information.

Bock, G. W., & Kim, Y. G. (2002). Breaking the myths of rewards: An exploratory study of attitudes about knowledge sharing. *Information Resources Management Journal, 15*(2), 14–21.

Clay, P. F., Dennis, A. R., & Ko, D. (2005). Factors Affecting the Loyal Use of Knowledge Management Systems. In *Hawaii International Conference on System Sciences* (Vol. 8, p. 251c). Los Alamitos, CA, USA: IEEE Computer Society.

Davis, F. D. (1985). *A technology acceptance model for empirically testing new end-user information systems : theory and results.* Massachusetts Institute of Technology.

Davis, F. D., Bagozzi, R. P., & Warshaw, P. R. (1989). User Acceptance of Computer Technology: A Comparison of Two Theoretical Models. *Management Science, 35*(8), 982-1003.

DeLone, W. H., & McLean, E. R. (1992). Information systems success: the quest for the dependent variable. *Information systems research, 3*(1), 60–95.

DeLone, W. H., & McLean, E. R. (2003). The DeLone and McLean Model of Information Systems Success: A Ten-Year Update. *Journal of Management Information Systems, 19*, 9–30.

Ebersbach, A., Glaser, M., Heigl, R., & Warta, A. (2007). *Wiki: Web Collaboration* (2. ed.). Springer, Berlin.

Fishbein, M., & Ajzen, I. (1975). Belief, attitude, intention, and behavior: An introduction to theory and research. *Reading, MA: Addison-Wesley.*

Goodhue, D. L., & Thompson, R. L. (1995). Task-technology fit and individual performance. *Mis Quarterly*, 213–236.

Grudin, J., & Poole, E. S. (2010). Wikis at work: success factors and challenges for sustainability of enterprise Wikis. In *Proceedings of the 6th International Symposium on Wikis and Open Collaboration*, WikiSym '10 (pp. 5:1–5:8). New York, NY, USA: ACM.

Holsapple, C. W., & Joshi, K. D. (2000). An investigation of factors that influence the management of knowledge in organizations. *The Journal of Strategic Information Systems*, *9*(2-3), 235–261.

Hsu, C. L., & Lin, J. C. (2008). Acceptance of blog usage: The roles of technology acceptance, social influence and knowledge sharing motivation. *Information & Management*, *45*(1), 65–74.

Hsu, M., Ju, T. L., Yen, C., & Chang, C. (2007). Knowledge sharing behavior in virtual communities: The relationship between trust, self-efficacy, and outcome expectations. *International Journal of Human-Computer Studies*, *65*(2), 153-169.

Klein, B. (2003). Assessment of information quality: Does the medium matter. In *Proceedings of the Ninth Americas Conference on Information Systems. Atlanta: Association for Information Systems* (pp. 2348–2352).

Kousetti, C., Millard, D. E., & Howard, Y. (2008). A study of ontology convergence in a semantic Wiki. In *Proceedings of the 4th International Symposium on Wikis*, WikiSym '08 (pp. 17:1–17:10). New York, NY, USA: ACM.

Kulkarni, U. R., Ravindran, S., & Freeze, R. (2007). A knowledge management success model: Theoretical development and empirical validation. *Journal of Management Information Systems*, *23*(3), 309–347.

Lee, Y., Kozar, K. A., & Larsen, K. R. (2003). The technology acceptance model: Past, present, and future. *Technology*.

Legris, P., Ingham, J., & Collerette, P. (2003). Why do people use information technology? A critical review of the technology acceptance model. *Information & Management*, *40*(3), 191-204.

Leuf, B., & Cunningham, W. (2001). *The Wiki way: quick collaboration on the Web*. Addison-Wesley New York.

Maleh, C. (2000). *Open space: effektiv arbeiten mit grossen Gruppen: ein Handbuch für Anwender, Entscheider und Berater*. Beltz.

Mason, R. O. (1978). Measuring information output: A communication systems approach. *Information & Management*, *1*(4), 219-234.

Morse, G. (2008). Conversation: Jimmy Wales. *Harvard Business Review*, *86*(4).

Nelson, R. R., & Todd, P. A. (2005). Antecedents of Information and System Quality: An Empirical Examination Within the Context of Data Warehousing. *Journal of Management Information Systems*, *21*, 199–235.

Oliver, R. L. (1999). Whence consumer loyalty? *The Journal of Marketing*, *63*, 33–44.

Poston, R. S., & Speier, C. (2005). Effective use of knowledge management systems: A process model of content ratings and credibility indicators. *MIS Quarterly*, 221–244.

Powers, R. F., & Dickson, G. W. (1971). *MIS project management: Myths, opinions and reality*.

Robey, D. (1979). User Attitudes and Management Information System Use. *The Academy of*

Management Journal, 22(3), 527-538.

Schaffert, S. (2006). IkeWiki: A Semantic Wiki for Collaborative Knowledge Management. In *Enabling Technologies: Infrastructure for Collaborative Enterprises, 2006. WETICE '06. 15th IEEE International Workshops on* (pp. 388-396). Presented at the Enabling Technologies: Infrastructure for Collaborative Enterprises, 2006. WETICE '06. 15th IEEE International Workshops on.

Seddon, P. B. (1997). A respecification and extension of the DeLone and McLean model of IS success. *Information Systems Research, 8*(3), 240–253.

Shannon, C. E., & Weaver, W. (1997). The mathematical theory of communication. *MD computing, 14*(4), 306–317.

Sharda, R., Barr, S. H., & McDonnell, J. C. (1988). Decision Support System Effectiveness: A Review and an Empirical Test. *Management Science, 34*(2), 139-159.

Smolnik, S., Urbach, N., Zimmer, C., & Raeth, P. (2009). Towards Assessing the Success of Social Software in Corporate Environments. *AMCIS 2009 Proceedings*.

Straub, D., Limayem, M., & Karahanna-Evaristo, E. (1995). Measuring System Usage: Implications for IS Theory Testing. *Management Science, 41*(8), 1328-1342.

Swanson, E. B. (1974). Management Information Systems: Appreciation and Involvement. *Management Science, 21*(2), 178-188.

Urbach, N., Smolnik, S., & Riempp, G. (2009). The State of Research on Information Systems Success. *Business & Information Systems Engineering, 1*(4), 315–325.

Venkatesh, V., & Davis, F. D. (2000). A Theoretical Extension of the Technology Acceptance Model: Four Longitudinal Field Studies. *Management Science, 46*(2), 186-204.

Wagner, C. (2004). Wiki: A technology for conversational knowledge management and group collaboration. *Communications of the Association for Information Systems (Volume13, 2004), 13*, 265–289.

Wang, R. Y., & Strong, D. M. (1996). Beyond accuracy: what data quality means to data consumers. *Journal of Management Information Systems, 12*, 5–33.

Wang, Y. (2008). Assessing e-commerce systems success: a respecification and validation of the DeLone and McLean model of IS success. *Information Systems Journal, 18*(5), 529-557.

Weaver, W. (1949). Recent contributions to the mathematical theory of communication. *The mathematical theory of communication, 1*.

Wu, J. H., & Wang, Y. M. (2006). Measuring KMS success: A respecification of the DeLone and McLean's model. *Information & Management, 43*(6), 728–739.

Yoon, Y., Guimaraes, T., & Clevenson, A. (1998). Exploring expert system success factors for business process reengineering. *Journal of Engineering and Technology Management, 15*(2-3), 179–199.